PASS THE PANDOWDY, PLEASE

CHEWING ON HISTORY WITH FAMOUS FOLKS AND THEIR FABULOUS FOODS

INTRODUCTION

Everyone needs to eat. Besides providing fuel for our bodies, food reflects culture, climate, time period, wealth, and beliefs. Whether we're enjoying food from a farmers' market, ordering at a drive-through window, sampling a dish from another culture, sharing birthday cake, or microwaving a prepared meal, our eating habits provide a glimpse into our customs and lives — and that was just as true for Cleopatra and Napoleon as it is today. History is written between the lines of menu items. Let's read the menu!

PASS THE PANDOWDY, PLEASE

CHEWING ON HISTORY WITH FAMOUS FOLKS AND THEIR FABULOUS FOODS

ABIGAIL EWING ZELZ

ILLUSTRATED BY ERIC ZELZ

TILBURY HOUSE
PUBLISHERS

COSMETICS FOR CLEOPATRA

Unlike the people she ruled, **Cleopatra** (69 BC–30 BC) enjoyed many food choices. Most of her subjects ate rough bread made with emmer, a hulled wheat flour, at every meal. Bakers kneaded the dough with their feet, and the bread was coarse enough to damage people's teeth. Ancient Egyptians also ate barley, vegetables, dates, and dried or pickled fish.

But Cleopatra also enjoyed lentils, walnuts, eggs, olives, and meats. Melons, pomegranates, figs, apricots, and peaches grew nearby, and she also snacked on treats sweetened with honey. During a trip to Rome she even sampled African snails, peacocks, and storks.

At lavish banquets with flowers, fancy foods, and entertainment, Cleopatra and her guests ate with their hands — no spoons or forks existed. And she dressed for the occasion. Crushed beetles and ants provided the red color for her homemade lipstick. Pickles were always close at hand; Cleopatra believed they enhanced her beauty.

I LOOK MARVELOUS!

I became an Egyptian pharaoh when I was 18 years old. There were other female pharaohs in ancient Egypt, but I was the most famous, the last, and I'd say, the most beautiful! I was a well-educated, witty, wealthy woman who ruled a prosperous land and knew how to get things done.

People say I once hid myself in a carpet that was delivered to Roman leader Julius Caesar, a future ally and boyfriend — but I'll never tell! Marc Antony was another Roman boyfriend.

They were both good fellows to know, as they ruled the powerful Roman empire. After I died, Egypt became a part of that empire. Ah, the things I did for Egypt! Can I help it if you're still talking about me more than two thousand years after my death?

TO MARKET WITH MARCO

Would you travel thousands of miles for pepper? Merchants and explorers like **Marco Polo** (c. 1254–1324) did just that.

Hard to believe? Imagine a meal with no spices for seasoning, and you'll understand how important flavor is. And what we consider common seasonings today were once exotic, expensive, difficult to obtain, and highly desirable.

The European meals of Marco Polo and his neighbors often combined tangy and sweet flavors and more closely resembled Indian cooking than modern European food. The city of Venice, Italy, where he lived, dominated the spice trade in Europe, with ships arriving at the busy harbor carrying spices from Asia.

Pepper, ginger, cloves, saffron, and nutmeg were valued for their health benefits as well as their flavor. Pepper was believed to cure ailments from heart disease to eye infections, and was sometimes used as money.

Do you like sugar on your hamburger? Cooks once considered sugar a spice and sometimes sprinkled it, along with nutmeg and cloves, on fish, vegetables, meat, and other savory dishes, all for the expanding taste buds of Marco Polo's world – never mind that taste buds wouldn't be discovered for another 600 years!

THE PLACES I'VE BEEN!

When I was 17, I left Venice with my father and uncle, who were merchants, and sailed east across the Mediterranean Sea. We continued overland through Afghanistan and crossed the Gobi Desert to reach China. I worked for Kublai Khan, ruler of the Mongolian Empire, for 17 years before returning home.

If I hadn't then joined Venice's war against Genoa and been captured, you might never have heard of me. During my imprisonment, I described my 23-year visit to East Asia to another prisoner. He enjoyed hearing of my adventures, so after we left prison, I published a book describing the people and places I had seen. *The Travels of Marco Polo* inspired later explorers, including Christopher Columbus.

DINING WITH DA VINCI

My most famous painting is the Mona Lisa, which I began in 1503 and worked on for several years.

Leonardo da Vinci (1452–1519) was one of the most gifted artists and inventors ever to have lived, but despite his amazing creativity, he may never have used some things you use every day: his own plate and fork!

In da Vinci's time, people ate with their hands as well as with knives and spoons. Because of this, they washed up at

the table both before and after meals. Not everyone had utensils, so diners would often share a spoon, simply wiping it off on their napkins before offering it to a neighbor. Da Vinci and his friends often sat in pairs at the table, helping themselves from serving dishes and placing their food on large, thick slices of stale bread, which absorbed the juices of the meal.

And although he may have been a vegetarian, da Vinci purchased meat for his assistants and servants. They ate two meals a day: a large, hearty one in late morning and a lighter one at dusk.

Any scraps?

Please toss them to the dog!

LET ME PAINT YOU A PICTURE OF ME!

Some say that I was a perfectionist and a procrastinator. I'll tell you later if that is true. I didn't complete many paintings, but I did fill secret notebooks with sketches and observations about people, plants, animals, and mechanical inventions.

To keep my notes private, I wrote backwards (with my left hand) in Italian from right to left, so my writings are most easily read by holding them up to a mirror.

Affluent dinner guests carried their knives with them.

CRISSCROSSING WITH CHRISTOPHER

When **Christopher Columbus** (1465–1506) sailed the ocean blue, he had to pack plenty of food for his crew — food that wouldn't spoil quickly.

Crossing the Atlantic Ocean took Columbus' ships about five weeks. The sailors were given one hot meal each day, which they ate from a single large wooden platter called a trencher. Their food consisted mainly of hard sea biscuits, rice, lentils, salted beef and fish, and any fresh fish they caught.

Because the sailors could eat no fresh fruit for most of their long voyage, many became sick with scurvy, a nasty disease.

Once in the New World, Columbus found many unfamiliar foods. He returned to Spain with avocados, guavas, maize (corn), chilies, tomatoes, beans, squash, wild turkeys, pumpkins, peanuts, papayas, and pineapples, which he described as "the most delicious fruit in the world."

In later voyages he introduced European foods to the New World, transporting oranges, melons, radishes, wheat, rice, barley, oats, coffee, sugarcane, and livestock on his ships. His cargoes of food helped change the eating habits of people around the world.

THE WEST OF THE STORY

You could say that I'm the kind of person who doesn't want to know when I'm wrong. When I sailed across the Atlantic Ocean looking for a western route to Asia, I thought I had landed in India, and I called the people I met in the Caribbean "Indians." But anyone looking at a modern map can tell that I was very wrong!

I spent time on ships as a young man, traveling with merchants to Portugal, West Africa, and other regions. I wanted to find a western route to India to trade spices, gold, and other valuables and become rich.

Although I made four trips to the New World, I never found the spices or gold I was looking for — but I found fame!

My sailors and I were afraid to eat some of the strange foods we encountered in the New World, so a taster back in Europe had the job of sampling them instead. If he survived, other people would know the foods were safe to eat.

NO MARSHMALLOWS FOR MOCTEZUMA

Imagine never having tasted chocolate! Until **Moctezuma II** (1466–1520), the Aztec emperor, hosted a lavish banquet for the Spanish explorer Hernán Cortés and his men in 1519, the Spaniards never had.

While feasting on tortillas, corn, roast duck, rabbit, turkey, and fruit as jugglers, musicians, and dancers entertained him, Cortés saw women bring Moctezuma gold cups filled with a frothy, spicy, bitter chocolate drink.

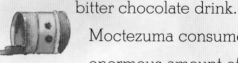

Moctezuma consumed an enormous amount of the chocolate drink, though it was not sweet like the hot chocolate that people enjoy today. It contained no sugar, but instead had chili peppers, corn, or even flowers added. The Aztecs believed that the cacao bean, from which chocolate is made, offered spiritual or health benefits, so they drank chocolate during religious ceremonies.

People used cacao beans as currency, but only the Aztec upper classes were allowed to transform it into a beverage and drink it.

When Cortés returned to Spain, he carried cacao beans so he could introduce this exotic drink to his friends at home.

It took nearly another century for people to perfect hot chocolate as we know it today, adding sugar and milk. Its popularity spread from the wealthy to all classes, even without marshmallows.

EVERYTHING GOES BETTER WITH CHOCOLATE!

If you were a powerful ruler, what special objects or privileges would you want?

I lived in a gorgeous palace surrounded by gardens with fountains and also had a zoo with birds and animals. I dressed in fine clothes, wore jewels and a feathered headdress, and had hundreds of servants.

During travels in my kingdom, servants carried me on a throne under a canopy decorated with feathers. When I stepped from the throne, they swept the ground in front of me and covered it with cloths so that my feet would not touch the ground.

I had all the chocolate I could drink, while others around me didn't get any. Chocolate drinks were only for special people like me!

WASHINGTON'S DENTAL DILEMMAS

George Washington (1732–1799) was the first president of the United States and also perhaps the president with the most teeth. But they weren't all in his mouth at the same time, and most of them were false.

Washington loved nuts. He bought hazelnuts by the barrel and blamed his dental problems on his habit of cracking walnut shells with his teeth. Ouch!

Washington owned several sets of dentures during his lifetime, which were held together with gold wires, springs, and brass screws. Chewing and talking hurt because his teeth fit poorly and made his lips protrude. And he had to speak carefully, because it was difficult keeping his spring-loaded teeth in place.

By the time he was president, only one of his teeth was real.

Maybe that's why he liked soft foods such as hoecakes (cakes made of fried cornmeal) with generous dollops of butter and honey for breakfast, or fish later in the day.

The bones, ivory, and teeth in Washington's dentures came from horses, cows, hippopotamuses, walruses, elephants, and even people!

The food and Madeira wine he enjoyed stained his ivory teeth, causing them to darken and take on a grained, wooden appearance, but contrary to rumor, he never had wooden teeth. And that's no lie!

I CANNOT TELL A LIE: MORE FACTS ABOUT ME

I commanded the Continental Army during America's fight for independence, and against all odds, we won! I became so popular that I was elected the first president of the United States.

I raised a lot of my own food at my Mount Vernon estate in Virginia.

I hired people and had slaves who cultivated my gardens and tended the chickens, sheep, and pigs. My estate included nut trees; apple, pear, cherry, and peach orchards; berries; wheat; and tobacco. I selected the site for the White House in 1791, but because it was under construction throughout my eight years as president, I never lived there. Although I died in 1799, you can still visit my teeth in museums.

Fast food for **Paul Revere** (1735–1818) and his large family meant cornmeal mush, a cereal-like dish that was also called hasty pudding because it cooked quickly in a kitchen fireplace. Revere often enjoyed it or ate bread for breakfast in his home in Boston's North End, but we don't know what he ate before his famous midnight ride.

Native Americans introduced cornmeal to the colonists, who sometimes called it Indian meal and used it to make bread, cornmeal mush, Indian pudding, hoecakes, and other dishes.

Other puddings that Revere and his fellow colonists enjoyed included baked carrot, squash, rice, apple, and bread pudding as well as boiled puddings, consisting of dough wrapped in a cloth and boiled.

Since the Reveres lived in the busy port city of Boston, they could buy molasses, spices, and other ingredients that arrived by ship. But they mostly ate local foods like fish, beef, pork, mutton, apples, berries, beans, corn, squash, and other vegetables. And want whipped cream on that pudding? The Reveres probably kept a cow that grazed on the Boston Common.

PUDDING FOR A PATRIOT

I WAS A FOUNDRY FATHER

Many people know that I rode a borrowed horse to Lexington, Massachusetts, late one April night in 1775 to warn people that British troops were on the move from Boston, but there's more to my life than that!

I learned silversmithing from my father and created, engraved, repaired, and sold a variety of gold, silver, and bronze items in my shop, such as spoons, buckles, and teapots.

I also made a famous engraving of the Boston Massacre and even learned basic dentistry.

After the Revolutionary War, I established a foundry with two of my sons. We cast bells that weighed more than a ton. Bells in church steeples and public buildings helped people tell time and signaled fires, funerals, meetings, and other events.

You could say I continued to alert people long after my midnight ride.

A
WAVE FROM
HOKUSAI

Would you like to eat the same food at breakfast, lunch, and dinner? Like his friends and neighbors, Japanese artist **Katsushika Hokusai** (1760–1849) ate rice at every meal. Breakfast might also include miso soup with vegetables, pickles, and green tea. At the midday and evening meals, rice would be served with lightly cooked vegetables, noodles, tofu, or simmered or grilled fish, which he ate with chopsticks at a low table while sitting on the floor.

A common evening meal was a bowl of cold leftover rice with hot green tea poured over it, accompanied by colorful pickles made from daikon radishes, cabbages, and a variety of other vegetables.

Like most Japanese people, Hokusai ate little meat, and he enjoyed fruit, sweet potatoes, and chestnuts instead of treats made with sugar.

IS MY ART ANY GOOD?

Do you ever think, "I'm just not good at that?" I was an artist in Japan, and although my artwork was popular, I wasn't confident of my abilities. Even when I was more than 70 years old, I wasn't sure my art was as good as it should be. But I believed that if I kept working, my skills would improve.

I created paintings and many paper prints from woodblocks. My prints were inexpensive (they cost about as much as a large bowl of noodle soup), and they were displayed in homes and decorated books, paper lanterns, toys, fans, paper snack bags, and other household items.

My assistants and I left our sandals at the door of my studio, where different blocks of wood were carved and inked on low tables set on *tatami* (straw) mats to make my colorful prints.

The Great Wave off Kanagawa is my most famous work.

In Japanese, the word gohan *means both "cooked rice" and "meal." When prefixes are added, the words mean* breakfast (asagohan), *lunch* (hirugohan), *or dinner* (bangohan).

A NAPKIN FOR NAPOLEON

Napoleon Bonaparte (1769–1821) preferred to eat alone. His servants would carry a table covered with food into his room, where he dined on several dishes at the same time — soup, dessert, the main dish, and other foods — rather than beginning with an appetizer and finishing with dessert.

Napoleon ate so sloppily that he sometimes needed to change into clean clothes after a meal. He ate no bread and disliked the strings in string beans, but he did enjoy roast chicken and pasta with Parmesan cheese. He even had a dish invented just for him! According to legend, his chef took food from a local farmer and prepared a dinner for Napoleon after his army won the Battle of Marengo in Italy. Napoleon thought the meal brought him good luck and ate Chicken Marengo often. The ingredients included chicken, tomatoes, onions, shrimp, and fried eggs — perhaps with a napkin for cleaning up!

My favorite coat

MORE ABOUT MOI

I was born on Corsica, an island in the Mediterranean Sea, in the year that it became a territory of France. When I was nine years old, my parents sent me to a French military school. After graduation, I became a lieutenant in France's artillery. I was a great military leader who won many battles and crowned myself Emperor of France in 1804.

Besides my military successes, I reformed the French legal, banking, and educational systems.

When I began losing battles and finally surrendered to the British at the Battle of Waterloo in 1815, they sent me far away, to the island of St. Helena in the South Atlantic Ocean, where I remained until my death six years later.

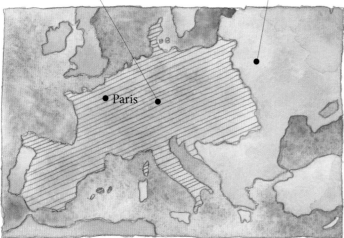

What belonged to me (and some pals) *What I wanted*

Paris

By age 26 Napoleon commanded the entire French army. He fought many battles in Europe, Egypt, and Syria, and expanded the French empire so it controlled a vast territory.

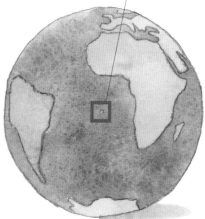

Where the British sent me when I was bad

FOOD FROM THE FOREST

What do you pack for a long camping trip? Trail food in the early 1800s didn't include granola bars, and finding food in the wilderness was challenging. But **Sacagawea** (1788–1812), the teenage Lemhi Shoshone who accompanied Captains Meriwether Lewis and William Clark's expedition, gathered edible wild roots, nuts, and berries for their group.

She dug Jerusalem artichokes, groundnuts, white apples (also known as prairie turnips), and wild licorice. The group also ate serviceberries, wild cucumbers, onions, currants, and plums.

Sacagawea's contributions made the meals healthier. The travelers consumed enormous amounts of squirrel, elk, buffalo, bear, fowl, deer, fish, beaver, and rabbits. They dried and smoked a lot of meat, transforming it into jerky to eat later.

Lewis and Clark had packed flour, sugar, coffee, cornmeal, salt pork, and beans for the long journey, but they needed to replenish their supplies along the way. They traded axes, mirrors, brass buttons, and other goods to the Native Americans they met in return for beans, corn, and other food.

A PEACEFUL PRESENCE

My name means "bird woman" in the Hidatsa language. When I was 17 and living with members of the Mandan and Hidatsa tribes, a group of explorers spent the winter in our village. They asked my husband, a French-Canadian fur trapper, to accompany them to the west coast, and they wanted me to go because I could translate the Shoshone and Hidatsa languages they would encounter along the way.

Two months before we began the journey, I experienced a difficult labor. Captain Lewis offered me a traditional Native American remedy of crushed rattlesnake rattle mixed in water. I drank it, and shortly after, gave birth to a baby boy.

For 16 months, my husband, baby, and I traveled with the explorers by boat and on land. Many members of our group experienced fevers, frostbite, bloody feet, and other difficulties.

The men loved my baby, and his presence (and mine) helped people we met along the way understand that our intentions were peaceful.

APPLES FOR ABE

Abraham Lincoln (1809–1865) was a great president, but not a great eater.

As a boy on the frontier, he ate vegetables and meat that his family raised. He also hunted and fished.

He liked bread with honey and would carry corn cakes to snack on while he read books during breaks from plowing or hoeing.

Lincoln especially loved apples, and ate them whole as well as cooked into applesauce, pie, pandowdy, and other dishes. (See the back of this book for a pandowdy recipe.)

At the White House, Lincoln breakfasted on coffee and bread or toast with an egg. Lunch might be a biscuit with fruit and nuts or cheese, accompanied by milk or water. Although he sampled dishes such as roast stuffed quail, salmon with anchovy sauce, champagne jelly, and meringue cookies at formal dinners, he preferred simpler fare such as chicken fricassee and oyster stew.

As president, Lincoln sometimes became so preoccupied with his responsibilities and was interrupted so often that he forgot or neglected to eat altogether!

I WAS FAIR, HONEST!

My start in life was humble. I was born in a one-room log cabin in Kentucky and later lived on farms in southern Indiana and Illinois. Because I attended school for only a short time, I borrowed books to learn about many subjects, including law. People called me "honest Abe" because I had a strong sense of right and wrong and tried to treat everyone fairly.

I grew to be about six feet, four inches tall, and looked even taller with my top hat. Perhaps I would have made a good basketball player, but that game did not exist during my lifetime. I excelled at wrestling and could swing an axe with great skill.

The people of Illinois elected me to represent them in state government and then in Washington, D.C., before I became the sixteenth president of the United States. I served as president during the Civil War, a time when the country almost came apart.

It was difficult for me too, and although my life had joy I also suffered much unhappiness; my wife and I had four sons, but only one survived to adulthood.

Even when sad, I could use humor to calm a tense situation. I loved to tell stories and jokes. I was finally feeling happy about the coming end of the Civil War when an actor fatally shot me while I was attending a performance at Ford's Theatre in Washington, D.C.

MAKE WAY FOR THE MONARCH

Guests who dined with **Queen Victoria** (1819–1901) rarely relaxed. The queen presided over formal, lavish meals served on fine china. But eat quickly or go hungry!

Queen Victoria ate fast, finishing a multi-course meal in 20 to 30 minutes. When she finished, her staff removed all of the plates, even if her guests had just been served.

Meals for British royalty and their wealthy friends included a lot of meat, potatoes, bread, rich sauces, and vegetables cooked until soft.

Fried ox feet, tongue, and sheep's head were popular. Poorer people consumed a lot of bread and cheese, but never with the queen!

During Queen Victoria's time, many new forms of silverware appeared in the homes of the elite. Do you use cake knives, fish forks, olive spoons and forks, butter knives, oyster forks, pickle forks, jelly servers, punch ladles, or asparagus servers at your home?

"WE ARE NOT AMUSED"

I reigned over the British Empire for a very long time. So long, in fact, that, like the dinosaurs, I had an entire era named after me, the Victorian Era.

I became queen when I was 18 years old. As a child, I frequently breakfasted outdoors; as queen, I sometimes continued this practice, and often ate meals with the windows open regardless of the season or weather.

I did not like jokes during mealtime. I ate fast and a lot, and became quite plump.

In 2015, a pair of my cotton knickers (underwear) with a 45-inch waistband fetched over $18,000 at auction.

We are not amused.

NO MEAT
FOR THE
MAHATMA

Do you enjoy Thanksgiving Day and its celebration of special foods? If **Mohandas Gandhi** (1869–1948) had visited the United States, he probably wouldn't have liked the holiday. Gandhi didn't eat meat, and he disliked the idea of eating more than necessary.

Like many people in India, Gandhi grew up in a family of vegetarians. He believed that avoiding meat was healthier for his body and soul. He enjoyed homemade whole wheat bread and drank goat milk, which he said gave him strength. He preferred raw foods because they used less energy to prepare than cooked foods.

Gandhi limited both the variety and amount of food he ate. He even stopped eating altogether on several occasions to draw attention to violence and injustice in his country. His fasts drew attention to events or policies he believed were unfair, and they sometimes resulted in positive change.

A PASSION FOR PEACE

You don't need to be big, strong, wealthy, or wear fancy clothes to be powerful. I know, because my simple life made a huge difference for millions of people.

I was born and raised in India and left home to study law in England. I practiced law in South Africa and then returned to India. I wanted to change some of the British laws that governed my homeland, which was then a British colony. But instead of using weapons, I organized peaceful protests to bring about political and social change. Through nonviolent methods, I helped lead the people of India in their struggle for civil rights and independence from the British.

My countrymen gave me the honored title of Mahatma to show their respect.

When I died, I owned ten objects, including a plate, bowl, pocket watch, a pair of glasses, and leather sandals.

A BELLYACHE FOR BABE

George Herman "Babe" Ruth (1895–1948) was a great major league left-handed pitcher and slugger between 1914 and 1935, and also a great eater.

His appetite was so tremendous that he often downed multiple hot dogs smothered in hot mustard, sauerkraut, or relish at the ballpark, washing them down with bottle after bottle of soda pop.

Babe ate large breakfasts and dinners too. Just as he amazed fans with his successes on the field, he astounded his companions by putting away generous helpings of steak, fried potatoes, salad, and apple pie with ice cream, along with lots of beer. It seems his home plate was often a full plate!

His huge appetite sometimes interfered with his ball playing. He gained and lost weight repeatedly and once was in such discomfort he was taken to the hospital. Whether it was caused by overeating or something more serious, his hospitalization was known as "the bellyache heard round the world."

BEFORE I WAS GOOD I WAS BAD

My parents named me George, but I got my nickname "Babe" when I was 19 and joined the Baltimore Orioles. The other players referred to me as the newest "babe," and somehow the name stuck. I later became a star player for the Red Sox and the Yankees, but before I was good, I was bad. I was born in a working-class meat-packing neighborhood in Baltimore, Maryland, and while my parents worked hard, I wandered around the neighborhood and got into trouble. I skipped school, got into fights, chewed tobacco, and even drank. Because of my bad behavior, my parents sent me to St. Mary's Industrial School for Boys when I was seven years old. People said I was "incorrigible." But then Brother Matthias, my favorite teacher, introduced me to baseball. I became really good at it!

DINING WITH DIGNITY

Everyone should be welcomed into any restaurant. But in the past, it was legal in the United States to segregate African Americans from whites at lunch counters and in restaurants, public restrooms, buses, and other places.

Lunch counters served simple fare like ham and cheese, chicken salad, bacon and tomato, cheese, and egg salad sandwiches as well as pie, coffee, and milkshakes. They also served up a lesson for a country struggling with fairness.

The **Reverend Dr. Martin Luther King, Jr.** (1929–1968), a Baptist minister and leader of the civil rights movement, worked to end segregation. He met with people in homes and restaurants, planning protests and marches over plates of traditional Southern food. He joined other protesters at a lunch counter sit-in in Atlanta, Georgia.

Dr. King traveled more than 6 million miles in his 13 years of social activism, giving speeches and organizing events. When he was on the road, he ate a lot of baloney sandwiches or canned meat with crackers. Sometimes he had to eat two dinners, because so many people wanted to invite him home for a meal.

Who could have imagined that these simple meals and lunch counters would come to play such a role in America's civil rights struggles?

I HAD A DREAM

When something is not fair, you can work to make changes.

Growing up, I saw that African Americans had to use separate water fountains and restrooms, sit in segregated areas in buses and public spaces, and attend segregated schools. I objected to these practices by leading a boycott of the city buses in Montgomery, Alabama, in 1955. Along with many other people, I also protested at lunch counters and other places.

During our peaceful demonstrations, hundreds of people, including me, were arrested. The protests sometimes became violent, but our actions helped to end legal discrimination.

In 1963, I delivered my famous "I Have a Dream" speech in Washington, D.C. The next year, passage of the Civil Rights Act outlawed discrimination, and I received a Nobel Peace Prize.

A MEAL FOR NEIL

Food crumbs and spills aren't a problem on Earth, but in a spacecraft they can float around and damage sensitive equipment. To avoid crumbs and reduce weight, **Neil Armstrong** (1930–2012), the first man to walk on the moon, and his fellow astronauts ate lightweight, mostly freeze-dried food that was prepared and packaged for their flight to the moon.

I WAS THE MAN ON THE MOON!

I always wanted to fly. I earned my pilot's license on my sixteenth birthday, even before I had my driver's license. When I began training to become an astronaut in 1962, my life became especially exciting. I became the commander of Apollo 11, and along with Edwin "Buzz" Aldrin and Michael Collins, I blasted off from the Kennedy Space Center in Florida on July 16, 1969. It took four days to reach the moon. When we got there, I climbed down the ladder from the lunar module and walked and hopped on the dusty surface of the moon. I broadcast the words that I'd composed earlier: "That's one small step for a man, one giant leap for mankind." Buzz Aldrin and I took photos, placed an American flag on the surface of the moon, collected rocks, and ran scientific tests.

Four days later we splashed down in the Pacific Ocean.

On the morning of the launch, Armstrong breakfasted on steak and eggs, toast, orange juice, and coffee. But once the Apollo 11 spacecraft left Earth, food came from color-coded foil-wrapped packages and pouches.

Using a special water gun, the astronauts squirted water into food pouches and then squeezed the rehydrated food into their mouths. Other space food was treated with oil or gelatin to reduce crumbs. Velcro tabs secured the food pouches in the spacecraft, preventing them from flying around the weightless interior.

Armstrong's first meal in space was rehydrated chicken salad, shrimp cocktail, and applesauce. After landing on the moon, he dined on bite-size bacon squares coated with gelatin, freeze-dried peaches, sugar cookie cubes, a powdered pineapple grapefruit drink, and coffee. That's one small meal for a man! When he returned to Earth, he was glad to remove his sweaty space suit and eat regular food.

IT'S ABOUT TIME!

69 BC
Cleopatra born in Egypt
30 BC
Marc Antony defeated in battle, Cleopatra dies, and Egypt becomes part of Roman Empire
410 AD
Rome conquered and conquering Visigoths

demand payment that includes peppercorns
Mid-1200s
Venice dominates spice trade in Europe
1254
Marco Polo born in Venice, Italy
1271
Marco Polo leaves Venice

on journey to the East
1275
Marco Polo arrives in the court of Kublai Khan, grandson of Genghis Khan
c. 1299
Marco Polo publishes account of his travels
1324
Marco Polo dies in Venice

1400
Pepper accounts for about 75 percent of all spices imported in Venice
1452
Leonardo da Vinci born in Anchiano, Italy
1465
Christopher Columbus born in Genoa, Italy

WANNA LEARN A LIITLE MORE?

CLEOPATRA

Egyptian women in Cleopatra's time were better educated and given more authority than women in other cultures. They held property, owned businesses, and became mathematicians, doctors, priests — and even pharaohs.

After Cleopatra became pharaoh, following the custom of the time, she was married to her younger brother to solidify the royal family's control. She ruled with him for a time, but later created an alliance with Julius Caesar and plotted to defeat her brother. When he died, she became the sole ruler.

A shrewd political strategist, Cleopatra further enhanced her power by identifying with the goddess Isis, whom Egyptians venerated as the divine and powerful mother.

Cleopatra is said to have made a bet with Marc Antony that she could produce the more extravagant feast. At the end of her sumptuous banquet, she dissolved a large, valuable pearl earring in an acidic concoction and drank it to win the bet. Scholars say the story is pure legend, but it added to her reputation for seeking power at any cost.

MARCO POLO

Spices during the Middle Ages played an important medicinal role. Europeans of Marco Polo's time believed in a system of "humors" that dictated which foods suited people's moods and health. They felt that spicy foods could energize lethargic people and blander flavors would benefit people who behaved rashly.

Contrary to what you might have heard, however, spices were not used to mask the smell or taste of rotting meat. Spoiled food would have made people sick!

Cooks ground up rock salt and crushed or ground whole spices such as peppercorns. During Marco Polo's time and for centuries after, salt was served in small containers called salt cellars. People took small amounts with their fingers or helped themselves using tiny spoons. Salt and pepper shaker sets did not become common on American tables until the early 1900s.

Did Marco Polo really travel as far as he claimed? Although some of his descriptions are fantastical, most scholars now agree that he did reach China.

1465
Bartolomea Platina composes first printed cookbook, which da Vinci owns

1466
Moctezuma II born in Tenochtitlan, the Aztec capital (modern-day Mexico City)

1492-1502
Columbus introduces wheat, rice, oats, coffee, oranges, melons, radishes, and livestock to the Western Hemisphere

1493-1502
Columbus introduces corn, beans, squash, potatoes, tomatoes, turkeys, chilis, avocados, pumpkins, pineapples, and other foods to Europe

1495
da Vinci begins work on *The Last Supper*

1502
Columbus's fourth and final voyage to the New World;

Moctezuma begins his reign and expands Aztec empire

1503 or 1504
da Vinci begins work on *Mona Lisa*

1506
Columbus dies in Spain

1519
Leonardo da Vinci dies in Amboise, France;

Moctezuma entertains Hernán Cortés

1520
Moctezuma dies in Tenochtitlan

1520s
Cortés carries cacao beans to Spain

1690s
Rice cultivated on plantations in the Carolinas in American colonies

1732
George Washington born in Virginia

1735
Paul Revere born in Boston

1759
George Washington marries and moves to Mount Vernon, VA

1760
Hokusai born in Edo (present-day Tokyo)

LEONARDO DA VINCI

Leonardo da Vinci was born in Italy — in the Republic of Florence — during the Renaissance, a period of heightened interest in the arts and sciences. Although he had little formal education, he developed wide-ranging interests and expertise in the arts, architecture, engineering, anatomy, and other subjects, recording his ideas and observations in dozens of secret notebooks. He sketched inventions that would not be built for several centuries, such as a parachute, a flying machine, armored weapons, and a robot.

At meals, da Vinci's friends and neighbors draped towel-sized napkins over an arm or shoulder and helped themselves from large serving dishes. Because of the Catholic Church's influence, many of them ate a lot of fish.

The word "companion" comes from the Latin words *com* [with] and *panis* [bread]. During the Middle Ages, people ate bread together, since slices of bread served as plates for food.

CHRISTOPHER COLUMBUS

Columbus introduced foods to both sides of the Atlantic Ocean, changing the way people cook and eat around the world. However, he and his men also unknowingly carried diseases to the Western Hemisphere. Because they had never been exposed to these diseases, the indigenous people had no resistance to smallpox, measles, scarlet fever, typhoid, cholera, chicken pox, and diphtheria.

Besides unleashing epidemics that decimated huge numbers of people in the New World, Columbus enslaved many of the people he met, forcing them to perform hard labor, and maimed others as an example to their peers. Many of the slaves he sent back to Europe died during the voyage.

If Columbus' sailors had eaten more local fruits and vegetables when they arrived in the Caribbean, they would have eliminated scurvy, a disease that causes weakness, swelling of parts of the body, loss of teeth, and other unpleasant symptoms. They mistakenly believed that their bodies would be unable to handle these new foods.

MOCTEZUMA

Central Mexico's Nahuatl language has given us words for foods that European explorers first encountered in that region: avocado, tomato, chili, and "chocolatl," the word for chocolate.

As ruler of the Aztec Empire, Moctezuma II consolidated the empire's control over its conquests of prior decades. By the time Hernán Cortés arrived, Moctezuma had ruled 17 years and was commanding tribute from 15 million people throughout present-day central and southern Mexico, one-sixth as many people as lived in Europe at the time. He had many wives — only two of whom ranked as queens — and many children.

To honor their gods and ensure the prosperity of their kingdom, the Aztecs made offerings of food, shells, jewels, and other items. They also sacrificed deer, snakes, dogs, other animals, and humans. Their human sacrifices, who included warriors, slaves, and children, received chocolate before being put to death.

Like Christopher Columbus and other explorers of the time, Hernán Cortés wanted land and riches for his country, wealth and fame for himself, and the chance to spread Christianity. It was a dangerous brew of ambitions. At first Moctezuma welcomed the Spanish as guests in Tenochtitlan, the capital of his great empire — near present-day Mexico City — offering them gifts and food. But the Spaniards' ambitions soon changed this peaceful interaction, and within months Moctezuma was dead. Some accounts say he was killed by his own people, others that he was killed by Spaniards, but it was Spanish designs on the New World that led to his death.

In subsequent conflicts, Cortés bolstered his few hundred Spanish soldiers with up to 100,000 warriors from tributary provinces that were revolting against Aztec rule. Cortés had horses, which the Aztecs had never seen, and cannons. And the Spaniards had smallpox, which reduced the Aztec population by half within a short time, killing the emperor who succeeded Moctezuma. After a prolonged siege and an assault in which his troops suffered heavy losses, Cortés conquered the Aztecs, destroying Tenochtitlan in the process.

GEORGE WASHINGTON

When his father died, George Washington, age 11, inherited the family's 280-acre farm and ten slaves. Later he bought and acquired many more slaves through his marriage to wealthy widow Martha Custis. At the time of his death, he owned 318 slaves. His will stipulated that they be freed upon Martha Washington's death.

Washington's teeth were bothering him by the time he was in his twenties. Many people of this time had dental problems because they didn't know how to care for their teeth and seldom saw dentists, who were rare and unskilled.

A handwritten book passed down through the generations of Martha Washington's family, *A Booke of Cookery*, contained recipes for dishes cooked over a fire. It has since been printed commercially.

PAUL REVERE

Paul Revere was a founding member of the Sons of Liberty in 1765 and one of the ringleaders of the Boston Tea Party, in which dozens of men on a cold December night in 1773 broke open 340 chests of Chinese tea aboard the British merchant ship *Dartmouth* and emptied them into Boston Harbor. This act of rebellion helped lead up to the American Revolution.

Henry Wadsworth Longfellow's famous poem "Paul Revere's Ride" doesn't mention William Dawes, who, like Revere, rode through the night of April 18, 1775, to warn colonists that British troops were on the march. Meeting in Lexington, Revere and Dawes rode on together toward Concord with Dr. Samuel Prescott, who was returning from a girlfriend's house when he met the other two riders. Only Prescott escaped a British patrol to warn Concord.

Paul Revere's participation in the disastrous Penobscot Expedition naval defeat of 1779 in Castine, Maine, damaged his reputation, but in 1782 he cleared his name at a court-martial.

In his foundry after the Revolution, he learned how to cast durable bells from an alloy that produced a pleasing sound. Revere's first bell apparently had a less-than-sonorous peal.

KATSUSHIKA HOKUSAI

Before and during Hokusai's life, Japan's ruling military class decreed which dishes the common people could eat, what clothing they could wear, and what sort of homes they could inhabit.

Japan remained isolated from Western contact, with the exception of the port city of Nagasaki (where the Dutch traded), until shortly after Hokusai's death. In 1853, American Commodore Matthew Perry, with threats of force, convinced Japan to open itself to Western trade. This sparked an interest in Japanese art, which influenced Western art and fashion, including Impressionist painters.

Hokusai's art decorated small paper bags used by street vendors to sell *mochi*, small cakes made from pounded glutinous rice, which people enjoyed on special occasions. These are not the same as the crispy puffed rice cakes familiar to people in the West.

1886
Coca Cola first made
1895
Babe Ruth born
1897
Jello-O trademarked
1901
Queen Victoria dies in East Cowes, United Kingdom;

Quaker Oats company established

1902
Necco conversation hearts introduced;

Barnum's animal crackers introduced;

Babe Ruth sent to St. Mary's Industrial School for Boys
1904
Peanut butter served at

World's Fair
1906
Corn flakes introduced by the Kellogg Company
1907
Hershey kisses introduced
1909
NAACP founded;

Electric pop-up toaster invented

1912
Oreo cookies produced by Nabisco;

The word "vitamin" coined; Prince macaroni introduced
1914
Refrigerated railway cars transport fresh produce to distant markets;

Babe Ruth signs with Baltimore Orioles baseball team and is then traded to Boston Red Sox
1916
First food guide published by United States Department of Agriculture (USDA)
1917
Marshmallow Fluff, originally called marsh-

NAPOLEON BONAPARTE

Napoleon started wars, conquered lands, and consolidated power by putting his relatives in powerful positions. He created the greatest European empire since the Roman Empire, and his brilliant battle plans are still studied. His Napoleonic Code — emphasizing religious freedom and rewarding workers based on merit — influenced law and society worldwide.

Canned foods first appeared during the Napoleonic Wars as a way to carry and preserve large amounts of food for soldiers. The handmade tin cans were secured with lead solder, which caused lead poisoning and required soldiers to use bayonets or other sharp implements to pry them open.

Are Napoleons, the multi-layered puff pastry treats with cream filling, named for Napoleon Bonaparte? Many people believe that the pastry name is actually a corruption of *napolitain*, a reference to the pastry's origin in the city of Naples.

In 1814 a defeated Napoleon was sent to the Mediterranean island of Elba, but he escaped the following year. He returned to France for 100 days and was then exiled to St. Helena. Although Napoleon's physician stated that stomach cancer claimed his life, rumors persisted for many years that he was poisoned.

SACAGAWEA

The Lewis and Clark expedition encountered nearly 50 Native American tribes during their journey. To each they attempted to explain America's acquisition of territory in the Louisiana Purchase (which doubled the size of the United States); that President Thomas Jefferson governed the newly acquired land; and that they desired peace. Despite cultural differences and misunderstandings, their encounters were generally peaceful, thanks in large part to the presence of Sacagawea and her infant son. "No woman ever accompanies a war party in these parts," wrote William Clark.

Sacagawea spent her childhood with the Shoshone Indians in what is now Idaho, and later — after being taken captive in a battle — lived among the Hidatsa people in what is now North Dakota. During her trip with the Corps of Discovery, while translating between the Shoshones and Capt. Lewis, she suddenly realized that the Shoshone chief was her brother, from whom she had been separated for several years.

Sacagawea received no payment for her contributions to the expedition. Her husband received cash and land, and Clark later financed their son's education in St. Louis.

mallow cream, concocted
1918
El Paso brand established in New Mexico;

Gandhi's first fast on behalf of striking mill workers in India
1919
Babe Ruth signs with New York Yankees;

Danone, later called Dannon, yogurt established

in Spain
1921
First radio broadcast of a baseball game
1924
Clarence Birdseye invents quick freezing method for freezing food;

Gandhi fasts for Hindu-Muslim unity
1927
Babe Ruth hits 60 home

runs in one season
1928
Bread slicing machine invented;

Bubble gum invented; Rice Krispies introduced
1929
Martin Luther King, Jr. born
1930s and 1940s
Electric refrigerators become popular, replacing ice boxes

1930
Neil Armstrong born;

Gandhi leads salt march
1933
Gandhi's longest fast, 21 days (for the improvement of the Untouchables' condition)
1934
Ritz crackers introduced

1935
Babe Ruth retires
1937
U.S. military rations include chocolate
1939
First television broadcast of baseball game
1941
M & Ms and Cheerios, originally called CheeriOats, introduced

---

Only one member of the Corps of Discovery died during the journey, when a ruptured appendix proved fatal. Records suggest that Sacagawea became ill and died in Missouri in 1812, though some believe she returned to the Shoshone people and died much later.

ABRAHAM LINCOLN

Although he personally opposed slavery, Abraham Lincoln believed his most important responsibility as president was to preserve the Union. He knew how the Civil War divided families and the nation. His wife, Mary Todd Lincoln, had grown up in a family that owned slaves, and her family members fought on both the Union and Confederate sides during the Civil War.

The Civil War began shortly after Lincoln's inauguration in 1861 and continued until 1865. About 620,000 people died — many in battle and from injuries, but even more from diseases.

In 1863, President Lincoln issued the Emancipation Proclamation, freeing slaves in ten Southern states. He also signed a proclamation establishing Thanksgiving as a national holiday.

Lincoln's family planted apple trees in Indiana, and he planted apple and other fruit trees on his land in Illinois. Apples are not native to America; European settlers introduced them to North America, and they became the most commonly eaten fruit in the United States. An apple pandowdy is similar to a crisp or a cobbler.

QUEEN VICTORIA

During the first decades of Queen Victoria's reign, her household staff placed many platters of food on the dining table at the same time. Later the custom changed, and servants carried serving dishes first to the queen, then to the other diners, who served themselves at the table. Small menus were placed on the table so guests would know what was being served.

During the mid to late 1800s, as cities grew and men worked away from home during the day, people began to eat their main meal in the evening instead of at noon. To ward off hunger during the long afternoon hours, an afternoon tea, accompanied by light sandwiches or finger foods, became a new tradition.

During Queen Victoria's reign, the British Empire expanded to include more than 25 percent of the world's population. Britain controlled trade with its many colonies, many of which gained independence during the twentieth century.

1945
Raytheon files patent application for microwave cooking system
1947
India becomes an independent nation
1948
Gandhi assassinated in New Delhi, India;

Babe Ruth dies in Manhattan, NY
1952
Cheeze Whiz introduced
1954
Burger King established;

Martin Luther King, Jr.

becomes pastor in Montgomery, AL;

Both Stouffers and Swanson & Sons introduce frozen TV dinners
1955
First McDonalds Restaurant opens;

Kentucky Fried Chicken opens
1957
Aluminum cans begin to replace tin cans for food
1959
Martin Luther King, Jr. travels to India and learns about nonviolent protests

1960
Martin Luther King, Jr. arrested at lunch counter sit-in in Atlanta, GA
1964
Civil Rights Act enacted;

Martin Luther King, Jr. receives Nobel Peace Prize

MOHANDAS GANDHI

For cultural, religious, and economic reasons, India has a higher percentage of vegetarians than any other country — 31 to 40 percent of the population versus a mere two percent of Americans. Abstaining from meat was part of his family's tradition, and Gandhi embraced vegetarianism even more wholeheartedly after reading *A Plea for Vegetarianism* by Henry Salt.

During his 21-year legal career in South Africa, he began working to end discrimination and help oppressed people.

One of Gandhi's acts of civil disobedience against British authority in India included thousands of other people. The British East India Company controlled the sale of salt, spices, nuts, and other resources. Gandhi embarked on a 240-mile march to the sea in 1930 to protest the British control of Indian salt production from seawater. He began the 24-day march with 78 people. Along the way, tens of thousands of fellow Indians joined the march. Although thousands of them, including Gandhi, were imprisoned for breaking the law, the march gave momentum to the Indians' goal of independence.

India became an independent nation in 1947. Gandhi was assassinated the following year.

BABE RUTH

St. Mary's Industrial School for Boys taught its students a trade so they could support themselves as adults. Child labor was still common during the first decades of the twentieth century, and George Ruth learned to sew shirts, but baseball offered him a much more lucrative career. During the 1920s and 1930s he became the highest paid ballplayer to that point in history. Nicknamed "Babe" as a rookie, he was later called "The Bambino" and "The Sultan of Swat."

Babe never completely outgrew his youthful bad behavior. He quarreled with his managers and behaved recklessly. He was also involved in several car accidents and was jailed for speeding.

He helped the Boston Red Sox win World Series championships in 1915, 1916, and 1918, but the Sox sold his contract to the New York Yankees after the 1919 season. The Yankees went on to win four World Series with Babe, but the Red Sox didn't win another for 86 years, a drought that superstitious fans called the "Curse of the Bambino."

What's the story with Baby Ruth candy bars? They first appeared in 1921, the year Babe blasted a new record of 59 home runs. The candy manufacturer claimed the candy honored President Grover Cleveland's daughter Ruth, but she had died 17 years earlier. Babe eventually hit 714 home runs before he retired in 1935.

1965
Cool Whip and Gatorade introduced
1966
Quaker Instant Oatmeal introduced
1968
Rev. Dr. Martin Luther King, Jr. assassinated in Memphis, TN

1969
Apollo 11 moon landing
1971
Hamburger Helper introduced;

Starbucks founded
1978
Ben & Jerry's ice cream made in former gas station

1988
Lunchables introduced
1989
Fresh Express bagged salads introduced
1990
Nutrition Labeling and Education Act establishes nutrition labeling on packaged food

1992
USDA recommends nutritional guidelines in food pyramid
2005
USDA updates nutritional guidelines with MyPyramid
2011
USDA introduces MyPlate
2012
Neil Armstrong dies in

Cincinnati, OH;
2016
FDA updates nutrition information on packaged foods

MARTIN LUTHER KING, JR.

As a boy in Atlanta, Georgia, Martin Luther King, Jr. skipped both the 9th and 12th grades, entering Morehouse College at age 15. He was a gifted public speaker.

King led and participated in many peaceful protests. The Montgomery, Alabama, bus boycott he led in 1955 lasted more than a year, while his speech at the 1963 March on Washington was only 17 minutes long. All his acts of civil disobedience raised awareness and led to change, though some of the protests were met with violence. He was jailed 29 times.

King's example inspired the lunch counter sit-in movement that began in 1960 in a Greensboro, North Carolina, Woolworth department store and spread to other cities. More than 1,500 African Americans were arrested at lunch counter sit-ins. White customers sometimes dumped ketchup, hot grits, and other foods on the protesters, but lunch counters were eventually integrated.

A portion of the Greensboro lunch counter is on exhibit at the National Museum of American History.

Some of the foods King enjoyed were rooted in Southern cultural traditions. A few had their origins in Western Africa, since the slave trade also brought rice, okra, and black-eyed peas to the American colonies.

He was still working for social justice when he was shot and killed in Memphis, Tennessee, in 1968.

NEIL ARMSTRONG

When John Glenn, America's first man in space, squirted applesauce from a tube into his mouth during a spaceflight in 1962, NASA learned that it was possible to eat in near zero gravity. There are now more food choices in the international space station than Armstrong and his colleagues enjoyed in 1969.

The night before the Apollo 11 launch, President Nixon cancelled his scheduled dinner with the astronauts in order to ensure that he didn't pass along any germs to them. That same concern dictated the men's schedule after they splashed down in the Pacific Ocean following the moon landing. The astronauts spent three weeks quarantined in a modified Airstream trailer to ensure that they hadn't picked up any germs or diseases.

Physicians checked them frequently while the bored astronauts wrote reports, read, watched TV, and played ping pong. The space program also developed many devices that people now use every day, including cordless tools, smoke detectors, and flame-resistant clothing.

WHAT ABOUT YOU?

How will you and your food be remembered in the future?

Food helps paint a picture, with knife and fork, of the times in which it is served. One day, many years from now, you may be featured in a book just like this one. What will be the story of you, your food, and your times?

WANNA READ A LITTLE MORE?

BIBLIOGRAPHY AND SOURCES

Albala, Ken. *A Cultural History of Food in the Renaissance*. London: Berg, 2012.

Albala, Ken. *Cooking in Europe, 1250-1650*. Westport, CT: Greenwood, 2006.

Albala, Ken. *The Food History Reader: Primary Sources*. 2014.

Ambrose, Stephen E. *Undaunted Courage: Meriwether Lewis, Thomas Jefferson, and the Opening of the American West*. Simon & Schuster, 1995.

Berzok, Linda Murray. *American Indian Food*. Westport, CT: Greenwood, 2005.

Bryson, Bill. *At Home: A Short History of Private Life*. New York: Random House, 2010.

Bryson, Bill. *One Summer: America, 1927*. New York: Anchor Books, 2014.

Bushman, Richard L. *The Refinement of America: Persons, Houses, Cities*. New York: Knopf, 1992.

Carlisle, Nancy and Melinda Talbot Nasardinov. *America's Kitchens*. Boston: Historic New England, 2008.

Carrasco, David, and Scott Sessions. *Daily Life of the Aztecs: People of the Sun and Earth*. Westport, CT: Greenwood, 1998.

Coffin, Sarah. *Feeding Desire: Design and the Tools of the Table, 1500-2005*. New York: Assouline Cooper-Hewitt, National Design Museum, 2006.

Eighmey, Rae Katherine. *Abraham Lincoln in the Kitchen: A Culinary View of Lincoln's Life and Times*. Washington, D.C: Smithsonian Books, 2013.

Elias, Megan. *Lunch: A History*. Rowman and Littlefield, 2014.

Ferris, Marcie Cohen. *The Edible South: The Power of Food and the Making of an American Region*. University of North Carolina Press, 2014.

Flanders, Judith. *Inside the Victorian Home: A Portrait of Domestic Life in Victorian England*. W. W. Norton & Co., 2005.

Freedman, Paul H. *Food: The History of Taste*. Berkeley: U of California, 2007.

Guha, Ramachandra. *Gandhi Before India*. Alfred A. Knopf, 2014.

Hansen, James R. *First Man: The Life of Neil A. Armstrong*. New York: Simon & Schuster, 2005.

Hess, Karen. *Martha Washington's Booke of Cookery*. New York: Columbia University Press, 1981.

Jacob, Matthew and Mark. *What the Great Ate: A Curious History of Food & Fame*. New York: Three Rivers Press, 2010.

Johnson, Kathryn. *My Time with the Kings: A Reporter's Recollections of Martin, Coretta and the Civil Rights Movement*. New York: Rosetta Books, 2016.

Krondl, Michael. *The Taste of Conquest: The Rise and Fall of the Three Great Cities of Spice*. New York: Ballantine Books, 2008.

McNamee, Gregory. *Moveable Feasts: The History, Science, and Lore of Food*. Lincoln: U of Nebraska, 2008.

Miller, Adrian. *Soul Food: The Surprising Story of an American Cuisine One Plate at a Time*. Chapel Hill: University of North Carolina, 2013.

Oliver, Sandra L. *Food in Colonial and Federal America*. Westport, CT: Greenwood, 2005.

Pollan, Michael. *The Botany of Desire: A Plant's Eye View of the World*. New York: Random House, 2001.

Polo, Marco and Morris Rossabi. *The Travels of Marco Polo*. Sterling, 2012.

Portilla, Miguel León, and Lysander Kemp. *The Broken Spears: The Aztec Account of the Conquest of Mexico*. Boston: Beacon, 1962.

Rath, Eric C. *Food and Fantasy in Early Modern Japan*. Berkeley: U of California, 2010.

Richie, Donald. *A Taste of Japan: Food Fact and Fable: What the People Eat: Customs and Etiquette*. Tokyo: Kodansha International, 1985.

Schiff, Stacy. *Cleopatra: A Life*. New York: Little, Brown, 2010.

Sitwell, William. *A History of Food in 100 Recipes*. New York: Little, Brown, 2013.

Smelser, Marshall. *The Life that Ruth Built: A Biography*. The New York Times Book Co., 1975.

Sokolov, Raymond, *Why We Eat What We Eat: How the Encounter Between the New World and the Old Changed the Way Everyone on the Planet Eats*. Summit Books, 1991.

Tannahill, Reay. *Food in History*. New York: Three Rivers Press, 1988.

Thompson, Sarah E. *Hokusai*. Museum of Fine Arts Publications, 2015.

Turner, Jack. *Spice: The History of a Temptation*. New York: Alfred A. Knopf, 2004.

Visser, Margaret. *The Rituals of Dinner: The Origins, Evolution, Eccentricities, and Meaning of Table Manners*. New York: Grove Weidenfeld, 1991.

Weintraub, Stanley. *Victorian Yankees at Queen Victoria's Court*. U of Delaware Press, 2011.

Zanger, Mark. *The American History Cookbook*. Westport, CT: Greenwood, 2003.

WEBSITES

airandspace.si.edu
foodtimeline.org
history.com
metmuseum.org
mountvernon.org
nationalgeographic.com
paulreverehouse.org
pbs.org
smithsonianmag.com

A TASTE OF HISTORY

Called Pandowdy or Pan Dowdy, there are many versions of this baked fruit dessert. Try this historic recipe or search online for a modern version.

A Nice Pandowdy

Pare and slice enough tart apples to fill a flat earthen or tin pan to the depth of two inches. To three quarts of apple add one cupful of sugar, a grated nutmeg, one cupful of cold water, and butter the size of a walnut. Cover this with plain pie-crust (have the crust about an inch thick), and bake slowly two hours and a half; then cover and set for an hour where it will keep hot.

Serve with sugar and cream.

From *Mary Whitcher's Shaker House-Keeper*, 1882
Collection of Hancock Shaker Village, Pittsfield, MA

ABBY ZELZ has worked in history museums and contributed to historical and educational publications. While she would enjoy sharing a meal with many of these people, she admits to a dislike of cornmeal mush.

ERIC ZELZ has been drawing and painting for as long as he can remember, and would love to have a meal with any of the figures in this book, as long as Marco Polo's camels were flea-free and Babe Ruth shared a hot dog or two. See more of his work at **ericzelz.com.**

Abby and Eric live in Maine with their daughter, Charlotte.

PHOTO CREDIT: CHARLOTTE ZELZ

ACKNOWLEDGMENTS

We are grateful for the encouragement of family members and friends, especially those at the *Bangor Daily News* and John Bapst Memorial High School. Special thanks to Charlotte Zelz, Kim Roberts, Sandra Oliver, Eric Duncan, Marilyn Zoidis, Jon and Mariellen Eaton, George Danby, Sarah Walker Caron, and the helpful staff at the Bangor Public Library.

passthepandowdyplease.com

TILBURY HOUSE PUBLISHERS

12 Starr Street
Thomaston, Maine 04861
800-582-1899
tilburyhouse.com

Hardcover ISBN 978-088448-468-4
eBook ISBN 978-0-88448-538-4

First hardcover printing September 2016

15 16 17 18 19 20 XXX 10 9 8 7 6 5 4 3 2 1

Library of Congress Control Number: 2016942604

Designed by Eric Zelz
Watercolor illustrations were done on Arches 300 lb. hot press paper, using Winsor and Newton paints.
The text type is Stymie.
Scanning and color balancing by Alan LaVallee, Visual Art Imaging, Thomaston, Maine
Printed in China through Four Colour Print Group, Louisville, KY

5-18-2016
67140-0
Printed by Shenzhen Caimei Printing Co., Ltd., Shenzhen, China